Inspirin

Wome

Every Day

May

MERCY-BRINGERS

·······································

NATALIE WILLIAMS

June

HIS NAME IS BETTER

·······································

EMMA SCRIVENER

MIX
Paper from
responsible sources
FSC® C021017
www.fsc.org

WAVERLEY ABBEY
RESOURCES

Natalie Williams

Natalie grew up in relative poverty in the deprived seaside town of Hastings. She became a Christian at 15, which changed her life completely. Natalie is the chief executive of Christian charity Jubilee+ and co-author of four books, including *Invisible Divides* (SPCK, 2022) and *A Call to Act* (David C Cook, 2020). She is passionate about the church being a place of overflowing mercy, especially for those trapped by poverty or injustice.

Emma Scrivener

Emma Scrivener was born in Belfast, but now lives with her husband and two children in the southeast of England. She is the author of several books, including *A New Name* (IVP, 2012), and *A New Day* (SPCK, 2017). Emma speaks around the country, is a Radio 4 contributor and has written various magazine and newspaper articles. She's passionate about sharing the good news of Jesus and blogs about identity, faith and mental health at emmascrivener.net.

Mercy-Bringers

NATALIE WILLIAMS

A few years ago, a friend of mine died in a traffic accident. At the age of 34, she was killed by a lorry driver as she was cycling to work. The driver was arrested for causing death by careless driving. He had not paid proper attention as he reversed around a corner, so did not see my friend despite other drivers and pedestrians trying to alert him. After pleading guilty, he was warned that he was facing a prison sentence.

But my friend's parents wrote to the judge before sentencing took place and asked him to show mercy. The judge relented, saying: 'They do not seek retribution and have recognised how this has affected you'. Isn't that incredible? I don't think I would have been thinking about how the driver was affected. I would be more concerned with how *I* was affected!

However, my friend's parents extended mercy to the man who caused their daughter's death. As a result, he didn't go to prison but was instead given a suspended sentence and banned from driving for three years. National and local media covered the court case. One headline read: 'Death driver shown mercy'.

The reason this story made national news is that this kind of mercy is so rare. Even the word 'mercy' is not commonly heard today. Mercy is loving kindness in action towards someone who does not deserve it. It is active compassion towards those who have no right to demand it and no reason to expect it. My friend's parents were able to show mercy because they had experienced mercy. Over this month, we will be exploring God's mercy for us and His desire for us to be mercy-bringers.

James 2:12–14

'Mercy triumphs over judgment.'
(v13b)

For Prayer and reflection

Lord, as I reflect on Your mercy this month, may I grasp the wonder of it and be shaped by it? Please let it transform my heart, my attitudes and my actions. Amen.

A God **merciful**

Exodus 34:2–10

'The LORD
passed before him
and proclaimed,
"The LORD, the
LORD, a God
merciful and
gracious"' (v6,
ESV)

Moses spoke boldly to God – asking to learn God's ways and to find favour with Him; reminding God that these were His people; calling on God to be with him. And then, in perhaps his most daring request of the Lord, Moses said, 'Now show me your glory' (Exod. 33:18). I wonder what Moses expected God to do. He wanted to see the glory of the creator of the universe, the mighty, awesome one who made all things. It sounds demanding, almost brazen. Presumably God could have responded in various ways. He could have roared like thunder and lightning. He could have flung some new stars into the night sky. He could have created a new animal right in front of Moses. He could have picked up a mountain and moved it.

But instead of moving a mountain, God Almighty invited Moses to come up a mountain and meet with Him. On Mount Sinai, God revealed His glory to Moses as this: I am 'a God merciful'.

Ponder for a moment how astonishing that is. God could have dazzled Moses with a display of His might and magnificence. God's glory can be seen in His power, His wisdom, His holiness. It is displayed through all of His attributes and all of His works.

But here we see that when Moses was getting as close to God as anyone could get before Jesus came, God's primary way of identifying Himself was as 'a God merciful and gracious, slow to anger, and abounding in steadfast love and faithfulness' (Exod. 34:6, ESV).

In this precious moment with Moses on the mountain, we find that it is God's merciful character that most reveals His glory. Our God is merciful. It is who He is. It is still how He reveals His glory today.

For Prayer and reflection

Thank You, Father God, that You are 'a God merciful'. Thank You for the mercy You have shown to me. Please reveal more of Your mercy to me today. Amen.

Rich in mercy

Ephesians 2:1–10

'But because of his great love for us, God, who is rich in mercy, made us alive with Christ' (vv4–5)

I t amazes me how easy it is to forget that God is merciful. I often come to Him feeling like I have to persuade Him to show mercy. I can frequently slip into an approach that sounds more like cajoling, nagging or arm-twisting than one that is rooted in a deep understanding that God is good and kind and loving towards me.

Our Father in heaven is not reluctant to be merciful. It is His nature, His very heart. We don't have to beg Him to show mercy. In fact, the Bible tells us that it is God's delight to show mercy' (Micah 7:18). He delights to pour out His mercy upon us. It thrills His heart.

When we first came to God, it was through His mercy. That is where we first meet with Him – at the mercy of the cross, where Jesus died for us though we did not deserve it and could not earn it. We were enemies of God, objects of wrath, and yet Jesus died in our place. With His blood, He bought our adoption into the family of God. He paid for the forgiveness of our sins. He ransomed us from the kingdom of darkness, rescuing us, redeeming us, and bringing us into His kingdom. God did not withhold His mercy from us. It was and is His delight to show us mercy. He is *rich* in mercy. He is not stingy with it. He is not tightfisted or hardhearted. He is openhanded and tenderhearted.

One of the hardest truths for me to hold onto deep in my heart, especially when life is difficult or painful, is that God is not mean, He is merciful. It brought Him joy to pour out His mercy upon you the day He saved you, and it has been bringing Him joy to show you mercy every day since.

For Prayer and reflection

Lord, thank You that we see Your rich mercy most powerfully in the death of Jesus on the cross for us. Thank You for delighting to show us mercy then, and now. Amen.

Relentless in mercy

Lamentations 3:21–26

'His mercies never come to an end; they are new every morning' (vv22–23, ESV)

I f you are anything like me, it can be relatively easy to believe in the mercy of God that reached out to me on the day I was saved, but much harder to believe that He still delights to show mercy to me now that I am a Christian who still sins and makes mistakes. Somehow, I find that I regularly fall into the trap of thinking that I should know better now, and therefore God's mercy is subject to how well I am performing as a follower of Jesus. But the Bible is very clear that God's mercy is dependent on Him, not me. In fact, the apostle Paul says I am 'foolish' when I start to believe that my 'works' can earn God's grace (Gal. 3:1).

God is merciful to me because it is who He is. His mercy does not wax and wane according to my behaviour. Mercy, by its very nature, is undeserved, unmerited, unearned. If I had a right to it or any claim to it at all, it would not be mercy.

We are told repeatedly that God's mercy is unending. Just look through Psalm 136 in the New King James Version to read over and over again that 'His mercy *endures* forever'. God has new mercies for us each day. I know that I need new mercies every single day!

With the coronavirus pandemic, I have been more aware than ever that nothing around me is certain. Our whole world can change in a moment. But God's mercy is steadfast – we can depend on it completely. It is fresh for us each day. As the author of Lamentations writes, 'this I call to mind and therefore I have hope' (3:21). My hope is not in anything within me or around me. My hope is in His relentless mercies, which never come to an end and are new every morning.

For Prayer and reflection

Thank You, Father God, that You have new mercies for me every single day as I walk with You. Please help me to grasp afresh that I can depend on You and have hope. Amen.

Wellbeing Books

Invest in your personal and spiritual growth with books to support your mental health and wellbeing.

God's Plan for Your Wellbeing

Bouncing Forwards

Your Personal Encourager

Christ Empowered Living

Every Day Insights

The *Every Day Insights* series seeks to help those on a journey of learning, supporting others or facing difficult situations or emotions themselves to be supported each day.

Visit the link below for more information
wvly.org/mhw

Crowned with mercy

Psalm 103:1–14

'Who crowns you with lovingkindness and tender mercies' (v4, NKJV)

The most precious crown inside the Tower of London is the St Edward's Crown. It is made of solid gold and weighs five pounds. It is only worn during the coronation ceremony for a new king or queen. A more 'everyday' crown is the Imperial State Crown, which Queen Elizabeth II wears on formal occasions. This supposedly less impressive crown is set with 2,868 diamonds, 17 sapphires, 11 emeralds, 269 pearls and four rubies.* Crowns symbolise status, power and authority. They are grand and ornate, reflecting the dignity and rule of the person wearing them. They attract attention – they are made to be noticed, to draw the eye in wonder and reverence.

God has crowned His children not with gold or diamonds, but with lovingkindness and tender mercies. We have been clothed with these as a precious crown; in the same way that a monarch's crown symbolises their relationship with their country and their subjects, so our crowns symbolise our relationship with God.

We have been saved and secured with lovingkindness and tender mercies. These adorn our heads now that we have been brought into God's family. Notice that as well as being rich and relentless, God's mercies are tender. He is compassionate towards us. His love for us is steadfast. He wants to do us good. He wants us. And as sign that we belong to Him, we are crowned with His tender mercies. God crowns us for His glory and our good, which is wonderful. But it isn't just for us. Like a precious royal crown, our crowns of mercy are meant to attract attention too. We'll be exploring this more in the coming days.

For Prayer and reflection

God, thank You for crowning me with tender mercies. As a diamond reflects the light, please help me to reflect Your mercy to the people You have placed around me. Amen.

*wvly.org/iwed-mj22-6may

Weekend

A wonderful invitation

....

Luke 6:27–36

'Be merciful, just as your Father is merciful.' (v36)

I started going to church when I was a teenager because I liked a boy. I wasn't looking into faith. I wasn't seeking anything spiritual. I just heard that the boy I had a crush on went to church, so I decided to go along to see if I could spend more time with him. I wanted to get to know him better but, to my surprise, I ended up getting to know God instead.

I was 15 when I became a Christian. At the time, I didn't know much about Jesus at all. I knew some Bible stories about Joseph and his colourful coat, David the giant-killer, and Noah filling a boat with animals to save them from a flood, but the truth is that I didn't really understand what I was signing up for!

Ever since that moment, my eyes have been – and continue to be – regularly and repeatedly opened to the extent of my sin. Rather than being overwhelmed by it, instead it reveals to me just how great the mercy of God is. Not only has Jesus shown me incredible mercy, paying the price for my sins, but here He extends this wonderful invitation to *me* – that I can be merciful just like my Father in heaven!

....

Optional further reading

Dane Ortlund, *Gentle and Lowly* (Wheaton, IL: Crossway, 2020)

Love mercy

Micah 6:6–8

'What does the LORD require of you? To act justly and to love mercy' (v8)

Have you ever held a door open for someone and felt annoyed when they didn't say 'thank you'? Or perhaps you have occasionally driven along a narrow road, pulling to one side to give way so that another could driver pass. If they failed to wave their hand politely to express gratitude, did it bother you? I'll be honest with you: little things like this irritate me. I love that Jesus invites me to be merciful, but I don't find it easy. It takes effort. However, if my church ran a discipleship course in how to be judgmental, I wouldn't need to attend. I don't need help in that area – it seems to come naturally to me! I suspect I'm not alone, and I wonder if that's why God has to tell His people to 'love mercy'. If we think about it for a minute, doesn't it seem odd? Last week we were dwelling on how merciful the Lord is to us. Of all the people on the planet, aren't we the ones who should most wholeheartedly love mercy?

Yet here, through the prophet Micah, God tells us that He *requires* us to love mercy. In my own life, I know that I have a tendency to love the mercy God has shown to me, but I am not always so keen on His mercy when it is shown to other people, especially if they don't seem grateful for kindness when it is given to them. Loving mercy is first and foremost a heart issue. This week, we will explore this through various characters in the Bible, some of whom didn't love mercy. We will learn from them that we cannot 'be merciful' (Luke 6:36) until we really love mercy for ourselves *and* others. That is what God is calling us to. It's what He requires of us.

For Prayer and reflection

Can you think of specific people – whether groups or individuals – who you struggle to show mercy to?

The **deserving**

'There is still a son of Jonathan; he is lame in both feet.' (v3)

Mephibosheth was five years old when he was involved in an accident that changed his life forever. He was in danger so his nurse picked him up so they could flee, 'but as she hurried to leave, he fell and became disabled' (2 Sam. 4:4). At that time, in that culture, Mephibosheth would not have been able to support himself independently. He would have relied on his family, who had now all been killed.

In today's reading, we see that David didn't know whether Mephibosheth was alive or dead until he starts asking if there is anyone left of Saul's family to whom he could 'show God's kindness' (2 Sam. 9:3). Mephibosheth was hidden away in obscurity when David reached out to him. He might have imagined he was being summoned to be put to death, as was common at the time. So when David promises him that he will restore his family's land to him and welcome him to the royal table for the rest of his life, Mephibosheth bows down in humility and gratitude for David's unwarranted mercy.

Imagine that someone like Mephibosheth comes to your church asking for help. Perhaps he visits your foodbank or debt centre saying, 'I am in need with no way to support myself. Please will you provide for me?' Maybe you would ask him to tell you his story. If he explains to you, 'I was in a horrible accident when I was five and I've been unable to walk, or to work, ever since,' what do you think would happen in your heart? My response to a story such as Mephibosheth's is compassion and mercy. He is a victim of circumstances. His situation isn't his fault. Therefore, I think of him as 'deserving' of my help.

For Prayer and reflection

If you imagine someone with a similar story to Mephibosheth asking you for help, what is your instinctive response?

The **undeserving**

Luke 15:11–19

'The younger son…
squandered his
wealth in wild
living.' (v13)

Yesterday, we reflected on how we might respond if someone like Mephibosheth came to our church or one of our mercy ministries asking for help. Today, let's imagine a different scenario. What if you were at your local foodbank, or even at a Sunday service in your church, when a man comes in begging for help? He looks bedraggled and filthy. He smells as if he has been living in a pig sty. 'I'm starving to death!' he says (v17). 'Please help me.' Just as we imagined yesterday, picture yourself asking him, 'What happened to you? Please tell me your story.' So the young man begins to explain to you that he was once very wealthy, but he really loved to party. 'I had loads of money,' he says, 'but it all went on wild living and prostitutes' (Luke 15:30).

What would happen in your heart when hearing *this* story? In my case, I have a very different reaction to the Prodigal Son's starvation than to Mephibosheth's situation. Here we have a young man who is in need owing to his own decisions. Far from being a victim of circumstances, the Prodigal's predicament is entirely his own fault. Whereas I would not struggle to feel compassion for Mephibosheth, I know I would have a very different attitude towards the Prodigal Son. What happens in my heart is that I tend to think about the behaviour of the person in front of me and conclude on that basis whether or not they deserve my help.

We see this outlook in our newspapers frequently, with headlines such as 'Half a million scroungers get benefits – and you pay!' Our society divides people in need into 'deserving' and 'undeserving'. As Christians, should we?

**For Prayer
and reflection**

**Do you think that
some people are
more deserving of
your help than
others? Where do
you draw the line?**

Jonah's **anger**

T he prophet Jonah had a very clear idea of who deserves the mercy of God and who does not. When God told him to take a message to the Ninevites, he not only refused but he ran off in the opposite direction. Jonah didn't want to deliver God's message, but we don't find out why until later in the story. He didn't want to go to Nineveh because he didn't want God to show mercy. In fact, the prophet's reaction to the mercy of God towards the 120,000 people in the city was that 'it displeased Jonah exceedingly, and he was angry' (Jonah 4:1, ESV).

What I find particularly shocking about Jonah's attitude is that it came after he had experienced the mercy of God for himself personally in an astonishing way! After trying to run away to Tarshish, he was thrown overboard so that the ship he was travelling on wouldn't sink in a storm. He survived by being swallowed by a huge fish. Inside the belly of the fish for three days, Jonah prayed, and God spared his life. Not only that, but God still wanted Jonah to be His messenger – He gave Jonah a second chance to obey Him and bring about His mercy. Somehow, there was a disconnect in the prophet's heart between the mercy he had received and the mercy God poured out on the Ninevites. Jonah was grateful for God's mercy to himself, while simultaneously despising God's mercy to others.

Jonah isn't the only one. We see it in the older brother's reaction when the Prodigal Son returns (Luke 15:28–30). It is on display repeatedly from the Pharisees. Even the disciples are the same, wanting to 'call fire down from heaven to destroy' people (Luke 9:54).

'That is why I ran away to Tarshish! I knew that you are a merciful and compassionate God' (Jonah 4:2, NLT)

For Prayer and reflection

Father, please help me to love the mercy You show to me *and* the mercy You show to others. Help me to not be like Jonah, but to be merciful like You. Amen.

Why study with us?

Integrating your faith and your studies: Your faith isn't reserved for Sundays and church. It's part of who you are, and how you live out your profession. All of our courses are underpinned by a Christian ethos and understanding. Be encouraged to integrate your faith into your course, and your professional life beyond.

Flexibility to suit your circumstances: Squeezing in study around your job, your family, and your 101 other responsibilities? We'll make it as easy as possible for you. You can enroll on a course that's taught part-time or online via distance education. We have campuses in Farnham and in Bradford to serve the south and the north of England.

Choose your level: Whether you're studying for the first time, or you're a seasoned academic, you'll find a course at the level that suits you. You can try an introductory course, study a Waverley Award, or delve into a Masters, and anything in between.

Tutors you can trust: Our tutors have years of experience in their fields and many have completed doctoral level studies. You'll hear our tutors on podcasts, or see them contributing to journals and academic discussion. You're learning from the highly-learned.

Learning in community: Join a cohort of like-minded people and be part of the community of learners. Whether you're learning online or in-person, you'll be in touch regularly with your fellow students.

Where you can study

Our vision is to equip people, wherever they're based geographically. That's why we offer courses delivered in the Farnham Campus, Bradford Campus and via distance education.

Farnham Campus

Waverley Abbey House, Farnham, Surrey

Come on site to study any of the courses in the Counselling and Spiritual Formation Faculties.

Bradford Campus

Church on the Way, Bradford

You can study these counselling courses on site in Bradford:

- Introduction to Christian Care and Counselling

- Waverley Certificate in Christian Counselling

- Diploma of Higher Education in Counselling

Distance Education

Study from anywhere in the world with our courses delivered via distance education:

- Contemporary Chaplaincy

- Undergraduate Certificate / diploma in Integrating Faith and Leadership*

- Postgraduate MA in Public Leadership*   *subject to validation

For more information on courses you can study, please visit
waverleyabbeycollege.ac.uk

Outrageous mercy

Matthew 9:1–13

'Go and learn what this means: "I desire mercy, not sacrifice."' (v13)

L ike Jonah, the Pharisees struggled with the mercy of God. Their displeasure at His mercy oozed out of them at every opportunity. They took issue with Jesus healing those who were sick and for forgiving people, and even with who He would sit down to have dinner with.

When I read about the Pharisees, I judge them. I side with Jesus, assuming that is what I would have done if I was there at the time. But the truth is, I would have been upset by Jesus too. I might have been excited to see Him heal sick people (even on the Sabbath) and I may have been pleased to hear Him forgive someone's sins. But I know I wouldn't have been so thrilled to see Him having dinner with Matthew the tax collector and his group of unsavoury friends.

To me reading this story today, the response of the Pharisees seems outrageous. But the reality is that it was far more outrageous for Jesus to eat with tax collectors and sinners. This would have been scandalous to the religious people around Him.

For Prayer and reflection

Lord Jesus, I am so grateful that You came not for the righteous but for sinners like me. You desire mercy. Please help me to be merciful to everyone I meet. Amen.

Do you find it easier to love the Jesus who sits down to eat with Simon the Leper (Matt. 26:6) than the Jesus who shares a meal with Simon the Pharisee (Luke 7:36)? Perhaps for you it is the other way around. To put it in a current day context, I know I would prefer to see Jesus eating with a homeless person than a wealthy politician who doesn't seem to care about the plight of those in need. Or to put it more starkly, I would rather Jesus only spent time with survivors of modern slavery than perpetrators. But Jesus, like His Father, is full of mercy, especially for those we might write off as unworthy.

The weightier matters

....

Matthew 23:23–28

'You have neglected the more important matters of the law – justice, mercy and faithfulness.' (v23)

Jesus calls His followers to lives of radical mercy. We cannot do this without first working on the attitudes of our hearts. If, like Jonah and like me, you find yourself more prone to judgment than mercy – if you recognise that you look at people's behaviour and categorise them as 'deserving' or 'undeserving' – Jesus invites us into a deeper understanding of the mercy we have been shown.

Observing religious duties is important but, as we saw yesterday, God desires mercy above sacrifice. Jesus set this out plainly for the Pharisees when He called them hypocrites. He knew they followed the commands given by God to Moses when it came to tithing, but He accused them of neglecting 'the weightier matters of the law: justice and mercy and faithfulness' (Matt. 23:23, ESV). God's primary concern for His children is that we become more like Jesus. It is what He predestined us for – 'to be conformed to the image of his Son' (Rom. 8:29).

It is only once we have a profound understanding of the mercy of Jesus that we can be radically merciful ourselves. His mercy is our starting place.

....

Optional further reading

Tim Keller, *The Prodigal Prophet* (London: Hodder & Stoughton, 2018)

The Father's **heart**

Luke 15:20–24

'While he was still a long way off, his father saw him and was filled with compassion for him' (v20)

While Mephibosheth and the Prodigal Son stand in stark contrast to one another, the father figures in each story act in exactly the same way. King David and the Prodigal's father are both looking out. David is seeking someone to whom he can show kindness – God's kindness (2 Sam. 9:3) – and the father of the wayward son sees him coming home while he is 'still a long way off' (v20).

Both father figures go beyond welcome to bestowing what is undeserved. Remember, Mephibosheth's grandfather Saul had tried to kill David on more than one occasion. In becoming king, David could have put Mephibosheth to death. But instead, David gives him back land that belonged to Saul. That's mercy in action. And David goes further still, committing to provide for and take care of Mephibosheth for the rest of his life, giving him a place at the royal table.

Likewise, the father of the Prodigal Son could have turned him away, accepted him as a servant rather than as his child, or made him prove how sorry he was before welcoming him back. But he acts mercifully, filled with compassion, giving the son more than he had before. It amazes me that the father of this party-loving son doesn't rebuke him for his wild ways, but actually throws him a better party!

What we see in these two Bible stories is that, in the kingdom of God, kindness and compassion have everything to do with the giver and very little to do with the recipient. The mercy of God is based on who He is, not on the object of His mercy. As Christians, we don't look at the person in front of us and ask if they deserve mercy. We look at Jesus.

For Prayer and reflection

God, thank You for the way You father me. Thank You for looking out for me when I was a long way off. Thank You for Your mercy, compassion and kindness to me. Amen.

The mercy **manifesto**

Luke 4:14–22

'The Spirit of the Lord is on me… he has anointed me to proclaim good news to the poor.' (v18)

esus is the 'exact representation' of God the Father (Heb. 1:3) so it should be no surprise to us that He started His ministry by reading a manifesto of mercy. Following His temptation in the wilderness, Jesus had returned full of the Holy Spirit and was teaching in the Jewish synagogues. When the scroll of Isaiah was handed to Him, notice that He found the specific part that He wanted to read aloud. He wasn't told which bit to read. He didn't pick it at random wherever His finger landed in the text. No. He 'found the place' deliberately – in launching His public ministry, He started by revealing that He had come for those in poverty, captivity and oppression.

Jesus often said, 'The kingdom of God has come near' (for example, Mark 1:15). In reading from what we now know as Isaiah 61, Jesus was revealing glimpses of what it means for Him to usher in the kingdom of God. When Jesus came, there was an invasion of heaven to earth. Often when that sort of language is used, we think of signs and wonders, of miracles and healing. And those are definitely part of what it means for the kingdom of God to be rolled out on the earth.

But often we fail to remember that a key aspect of the kingdom coming – of God's will being done on earth as it is in heaven – is that the gospel is good news for those in poverty. Jesus was anointed not just to meet people at their point of crisis, though He absolutely did that. But He was also anointed by the Spirit to lift people up out of their poverty. And so are we. It is a vital part of bringing the kingdom of God to those around us.

For Prayer and reflection

What do you think it means, practically speaking, to be anointed by the Spirit to proclaim good news to those in poverty?

Stories of mercy

Luke 14:7–24

'When you give a banquet, invite the poor… and you will be blessed.' (vv13–14)

When we pay close attention to the Gospels, we find mercy everywhere. We see it in the stories Jesus told. In the parable of the Good Samaritan, for example, Jesus helps the expert in the law to see that loving our neighbour is about showing mercy that transcends all barriers. The road from Jerusalem to Jericho was a steep descent of about 17 miles, some of which ran through rocky, desert territory. It is interesting that Jesus makes a point of mentioning the route, but doesn't comment on the fact that the man should have probably known better than to walk a route that was notoriously dangerous for lone travellers. After telling the story, Jesus asks the expert in the law which man was a neighbour to the beaten man. He answers, 'The one who had mercy on him,' to which Jesus replies, 'Go and do likewise' (Luke 10:37). On another occasion, Jesus made it clear that there is a direct correlation between the mercy we show to others and how we treat Jesus Himself (Matt. 25:31–45).

Some of the stories of mercy Jesus told would have provoked uproar. When I read about the vineyard owner who paid everyone equally, whether they worked all day or just one hour, I feel a little indignant. It doesn't seem fair. Yet Jesus makes the point that the owner is free to be as merciful and generous as He wishes, and no one has a right to resent it (Matt. 20:1–16). In fact, Jesus calls us to be similarly generous. When telling parables about banquets, He says we should invite those others would not invite, those who cannot repay us (Luke 14:1–24). Many of the parables Jesus told are laced with the mercy of God.

For Prayer and reflection

Jesus, You made it clear through the stories You told and the words You spoke that we are to be merciful. Help us to cultivate this in our lives. Amen.

The **company** Jesus kept

'If this man were a prophet, he would know who is touching him and what kind of woman she is' (v39)

I n the Gospels, we not only see the mercy of God in the stories Jesus told but also in the company He kept. It is clear that Jesus spent much of His time with those in chronic need, and that He expended a huge amount of emotional and spiritual energy meeting those needs.

There seem to be no barriers to do with age, gender or ethnicity when it comes to God's mercy. Jews and Gentiles came to Jesus. Samaritans – hated by others – were not excluded by Him. Men were not favoured above women. Children were welcomed as just as worthy of Jesus' attention as adults.

Jesus interacted with those on the margins of society – the prostitutes, the 'unclean' lepers, shunned beggars, ostracised tax collectors, Roman soldiers responsible for oppressing the Jewish people. Those despised by everyone else were shown mercy by Jesus. In fact, those people no one else associated with not only felt comfortable with Jesus, they actively sought Him out!

Jesus seemed to extend His mercy to all of humanity. Not everyone responded with gratitude or with faith, but no one was turned away by Jesus on the grounds of who they were or what they had previously been or done. He wasn't oblivious to the sins and circumstances of those around Him – far from it. But He acted in accordance with His character at all times, rather than reacting to others. He knew exactly who He was eating with, touching, healing, forgiving. He chose to be a friend of sinners (v34). Like His Father, Jesus delights to show mercy to those most people would disregard and consider of little worth.

For Prayer and reflection

Jesus, thank You that You spent so much of Your time on earth with people others would reject and discard. I am grateful that You choose people like me. Amen.

'Tis **mercy** all

'He got up and rebuked the wind and the raging waters; the storm subsided, and all was calm.' (v24)

Through the stories Jesus told and the company He kept, we see His astonishing mercy for all who came to Him, and particularly towards those who were shunned by everyone else. But in the Gospels there is mercy to be found in less obvious places too. The truth is that the mercy of God is woven into every miracle Jesus performed. Every act of power is infused with His heart of mercy. Let me offer some examples.

When Jesus fed the multitudes, we are told that He had compassion on them because they were hungry (Matt. 15:32). He had mercy on them. He could have whittled down the numbers by weeding out those who had been around Him enough to know they should've brought some food with them. But He didn't tell the disciples to check who had the means to sort themselves out, or even to try to figure out which people were just there to see a miracle and had no real interest in following Jesus. He fed them all, because they were hungry and He is merciful.

When Jesus healed those who were sick, again and again we read that He was moved with compassion. What's more, we see that Jesus healed regardless of whether or not He was thanked (Luke 17:11–16). He had mercy on them all. When Jesus turned the water into wine at the wedding in Cana, it was an act of mercy to spare the bridegroom's shame (John 2:10). When Jesus calmed the storm, He didn't do it so that the boat wouldn't sink. He didn't need to do it to stop the disciples from drowning. It displayed His power and authority, but it was also an act of mercy to calm their fears. Mercy was entwined with power in every wonder Jesus performed.

For Prayer and reflection

Can you think of times in your own life when God has moved in power because He is merciful towards you?

Weekend

Blessed are the merciful

....

Matthew 5:1–12

'Blessed are the merciful, for they will be shown mercy.' (v7)

We are saved by grace, not by works, but curiously there are promises connected to how merciful we are, especially to those trapped by poverty or injustice. Jesus says plainly in our key verse that those who are merciful will be shown mercy. Another passage of Scripture helps us to put flesh on the bones of this statement. In Isaiah 58, we are told not only what mercy looks like in action, but also of the promises we can take hold of when we act in accordance with God's heart.

Mercy in action – or 'religion that God our Father accepts', as James calls it (1:27) – is expressed in taking care of those in need, especially those who have no means to take care of themselves. It includes practical support, such as providing food, clothing and shelter. But it also involves tackling injustice so that the oppressed can be set free (Isa. 58:6–7).

There are some glorious promises attached to this: God promises to heal us, protect us, lighten our darkness, guide us, satisfy us, strengthen us, and rebuild us even as we rebuild others (Isa. 58:8–12). He promises to bless us with mercy when we are merciful.

....

Optional further reading

Natalie Williams and Paul Brown, *Invisible Divides: Class, Culture and Barriers to Belonging in the Church* (London: SPCK, 2022)

Cultivating mercy

**Matthew
25:31–45**

'Whatever you did
for one of the least
of these brothers
and sisters of mine,
you did for me.'
(v40)

W e don't become more merciful, more compassionate or more kind by osmosis. We need to be intentional about cultivating these attributes in our hearts. Our actions won't change until our attitudes align with God's. It is only then that we become more and more like Jesus.

One of the ways I have found that I can cultivate mercy in my heart is by hearing people's stories. When I listen to someone talk about their life, their experiences, their trials and their triumphs, it creates space for God to develop compassion in my heart.

This particularly struck me on a trip to San Francisco. I was wandering around on my own, asking God to speak to me about this whole subject of mercy, specifically in regard to the idea of 'deserving' and 'undeserving' poor people. As I was walking and praying, I turned a corner and saw a man holding a cardboard sign that read: 'Why lie? I want beer.' Intrigued, especially in light of the prayer I had just prayed, I asked the man about his sign, and whether it might make some people think he was undeserving of their money. He began to tell me his story. Years of drug addiction had wrecked all of his relationships, he said. He'd received help and support, but each time he had left rehab he had quickly fallen back into his old patterns. He explained that in the last couple of years he had kicked his addiction to crack cocaine, but had 'replaced it with a new poison': alcohol. As he shared his story, instead of judging him for wanting money for beer, I began to feel mercy towards him. Listening provided a platform for my heart to be changed.

**For Prayer
and reflection**

**Holy Spirit, I invite
You to work in my
life over this
coming week and
beyond, that I
might cultivate a
heart of mercy in
increasing
measure. Amen.**

Merciful with **money**

1 John 3:16–24

'How can the love of God be in that person?' (v17)

I f we really pursue God's heart of mercy so that we can reflect Him to those around us, it will affect our wallets. I am deeply challenged by how John Wesley, one of the great preachers of the eighteenth century, handled his money. Wesley felt moved by God to see how much of his income he could give away to those who were poor. When he was 28 years old, he earned £30 that year. He kept the £28 he needed to live on, and gave away the remaining £2. The next year, his income doubled but he saw no need for his expenditure to follow suit, so he still kept £28, this time giving away the £32 that was left.

Once again, Wesley's income rose significantly. He earned £90, and gave away £62. The highest amount Wesley earned in a single year was £1,400. He still kept just what he needed to live on – this time £30 – and gave away the rest.

Challenging, isn't it? How many of us, under similar circumstances, choose to adjust our lifestyle instead of ploughing our excess income into mercy? When I first heard about how Wesley gave so much to those in poverty, I reasoned with myself that I am a good steward, and relatively generous. But provoked by a friend in my church, I looked through my bank statements for the last two months and realised that at least a quarter of my income during that time was spent on things that could not be considered essential. Perhaps that's not too bad, but then I asked myself this: 'Is it ever OK for me to have way more than I need when people around me don't have the basics they need?' If God's answer is 'no' – as I suspect it is – then I need to be more merciful with my money.

For Prayer and reflection

Over the last few months, do you know how much of your money has been spent on essentials compared to luxuries, or given away?

Breaking **materialism**

**Hebrews
13:5–16**

'And do not forget
to do good and to
share with others'
(v16)

I n the West, we live in a massively materialistic society, where it is common for us to spend money that is not ours. The pursuit of money and possessions is rife, and Christians are not immune from it. A few years ago, a friend told me that one day he opened his wardrobe and realised he had a problem: he noticed how many branded items of clothing he owned, including dozens of T-shirts he had rarely or never worn. Then he started thinking about how much money he spent on pairs of trainers.

My friend felt the gentle conviction of the Holy Spirit and realised materialism had a grip on his heart. When he asked God what he should do about it, he felt that he should only buy things if he could afford to buy two – one for himself, one to give away.

For a whole year, he applied this to everything he bought. If he picked up a cup of coffee on his way to work, he would buy one for someone else – blessing either a stranger in the queue behind him, or a colleague or a friend. When he bought a cinema ticket, the same principle applied. When he visited a supermarket to shop for food, he purchased two of everything.

That year was the first in a long while where he didn't spend upwards of £200 on a pair of trainers! By the end of it, the hold of money and possessions had been broken, and as a result my friend had been more merciful with his money than ever before. More importantly, a lifestyle of giving away was embedded in his heart. A sober assessment of our own materialism opens the door for us to make sure that possessions and comfort are not more valuable to us than showing mercy to people in need.

Merciful with **meals**

**Nehemiah
5:1–19**

'A hundred and
fifty Jews and
officials ate at my
table' (v17)

Jesus was perfectly happy to eat with a wide range of people, but for many of us in western cultures today we view our homes as places where we get away from the outside world, rather than welcoming all sorts of people in. This has been exacerbated during the pandemic, when various lockdowns have meant that we have no choice but to keep people out. We have already seen that Jesus ate with those who were rich and poor. He fed the crowds and he picked out people such as Zacchaeus the tax collector, inviting Himself for dinner. He ate with those who He knew would deny Him and betray Him. He ate with those who wished Him harm, and with those who loved Him.

Being welcomed into people's homes for meals has been a key part of my own story. I grew up in a working-class family in relative poverty. The first time I saw food served in separate dishes for meat, vegetables and potatoes was after I became a Christian. Though I didn't really know the rules for eating meals like this, it meant a lot to be welcomed into people's homes. Even today, as a single woman, one of the primary ways I experience the mercy of God through my church family is at the dinner table. In 2019, I went 46 days in a row being fed by friends.

Nehemiah spoke up on behalf of the people when they needed food, but he also fed people at his own table. It speaks volumes to people when we share a meal together, because eating with people is about more than food. It's about community, friendship and belonging. Our meal tables can be powerful places where people who feel broken, alone, ashamed or in need can find deep mercy.

**For Prayer
and reflection**

Who can you invite to share a meal with you? Think of someone who is outside of your usual circle of friends.

Proximity to **poverty**

Hebrews 13:1–3

'Do not forget to show hospitality to strangers' (v2)

When Martin Charlesworth and I were carrying out research for our first book, *The Myth of the Undeserving Poor,* we found that, even for Christians, our attitudes to poverty tend to be shaped more by our political preferences, media consumption and proximity to poverty than by what we read in the Bible. Continuing our theme from yesterday, one of the reasons eating with people is so important is because it opens us up to forming friendships with others. When we get to know people – when we eat together and hear each other's stories – our preconceived ideas can be challenged. God can work in our hearts to dislodge prejudices and faulty thinking about others, whether that concerns individuals or groups of people.

I know that my life is enriched by spending time with people who are not like me. I learn so much from others, especially those whose life experiences are very different to my own. I wonder if this is why Jesus chose disciples who were unlikely to get on well, naturally speaking. The chances are that Peter the fisherman and Matthew the tax collector would not have been friends if Jesus hadn't put them side by side for three years as they followed Him.

It is hard to hold onto certain views about people from other nations coming to our own 'to take our jobs' when you have spent time with a teacher from Bulgaria who tells you all about his meagre salary in his homeland, and how he couldn't support his children on what he was earning. Proximity to people who are different to us provides another opportunity for us to grow in mercy towards others. Understanding develops compassion.

For Prayer and reflection

Father, please bring me into contact with people who are different to me. Help me to learn from others, and to become more merciful as a result. Amen.

Weekend

Beyond crisis

....

Luke 17:11–16

'As they went, they were cleansed. One of them, when he saw he was healed, came back' (vv14–15)

Jesus met people's immediate needs before He met their deepest need. In fact, reading through the Gospels, it seems that sometimes people walked away from Him without having their deepest need met. Yet Jesus didn't shy away from helping people at their point of crisis, even if they didn't respond by placing their faith in Him as their Lord and Saviour. Of course, Jesus wanted everyone to come to know Him, and be saved. And we should take every opportunity to tell people about how wonderful Jesus is, and that He is the answer to our deepest need, and our every need. But it is important that we show mercy to people even when we cannot share Jesus with them. That is part of being like Christ.

Nevertheless, God's vision for people – especially for those trapped by poverty or injustice, those who are vulnerable, marginalised or oppressed – goes beyond crisis support. He cares deeply about economic and relational poverty, but He wants to deal with our spiritual poverty too. The ultimate expression of God's mercy is an utterly transformed life.

....

Optional further reading

Martin Charlesworth and Natalie Williams, *A Call to Act* (Brighton, E Sussex: David C Cook, 2020)

Oaks of **righteousness**

Isaiah 61:1–4

'They will be called oaks of righteousness' (v3)

The mercy of God in our lives turns us into mercy-bringers. We have the amazing privilege of reflecting God's heart to those around us. When Isaiah prophesied about the Spirit anointing Jesus – and us – to bring good news to those in poverty, in chains and in mourning, the story doesn't end there. God has a greater vision for the captives, the prisoners and those in poverty. A glorious exchange takes place where we are not only rescued but we are robed. In place of our ashes, we receive a crown of beauty. Instead of a spirit of despair, we are given a garment of praise. Where we wore mourning in our souls, we are now revived with the oil of joy. When God takes hold of our lives, we are transformed into 'oaks of righteousness, a planting of the LORD for the display of his splendour' (v3).

As if this wasn't wonderful enough, the effect of His mercy on us is not just that we bring Him glory but also that we do others good. We are lifted out of our brokenness so that we can become those who rebuild others. Isaiah says we will become those who 'rebuild', 'restore' and 'renew' (v4). This means we can expect to be a blessing to those around us – not just individuals we come into contact with but our communities as a whole.

I grew up in relative poverty in Hastings, on the south coast of England, which was once called 'Hell-on-sea' by a national newspaper. The promise of God through the prophet Isaiah is that the good news is for people like me, and once I've received it I can play a part in restoring 'the places long devastated' – deprived communities like Hastings that others might write off.

For Prayer and reflection

Thank You, Father God, that You have saved me and are growing me into an oak of righteousness. Help me to bring glory to Your name and do others good. Amen.

A **lifelong** journey

Matthew 5:13–16

'That they may see your good deeds and glorify your Father in heaven.' (v16)

By the incredible mercy of God that is poured out on us, we are transformed into those who can pour out mercy on others. When we consider that the mercy given to us was and is completely unmerited, it empowers us to move beyond asking whether or not someone deserves our kindness and compassion. Instead of looking at the person in front of us, we look up. We look to the example Jesus has given us, and we begin to 'be merciful, just as [our] Father is merciful' (Luke 6:36) even, as it says in the verse before, being 'kind to the ungrateful and wicked'.

Perhaps you're wondering where to begin. Ask God to bring people across your path even this week who you can show mercy to. Be prepared for Him to push you out of your comfort zone! When a friend of mine started praying like this, she found herself bursting into tears while out running when she passed someone sleeping on the streets. Prompted by the Holy Spirit, she ran home, made a bacon roll and ran back to give it to the person. For the next three years, once a week she would give out up to a dozen breakfasts on her morning run. For you, it might be harder still. Perhaps God will highlight that family member who drives you to despair, and ask you to cultivate mercy for him or her.

Look for ways to join in with others, too, because we are sharpened when we work together. If your church runs a mercy ministry such as a night shelter or foodbank or clothing store, how can you get involved? Can you offer some time, your skills, encouragement or prayers?

God has called us to be mercy-bringers. Don't delay. Press into it today.

For Prayer and reflection

Father, please help me to be a mercy-bringer. I want to be like You, showing mercy so that people will see my good deeds and, through them, see You. Amen.

EACH OF US HAS A NAME

Each of us has a name given by God
and given by our parents

Each of us has a name given by our stature and our smile
and given by what we wear

Each of us has a name given by the mountains
and given by our walls

Each of us has a name given by the stars
and given by our neighbors

Each of us has a name given by our sins
and given by our longing

Each of us has a name given by our enemies
and given by our love

Each of us has a name given by our celebrations
and given by our work

Each of us has a name given by the seasons
and given by our blindness

Each of us has a name given by the sea
and given by our death.

(Zelda, *Each of Us Has a Name*, adapted by Marcia Falk in The Book of Blessings: New Jewish Prayers for Daily Life, the Sabbath, and the New Moon (New York: Harper Collins, 1996) pp106ff)

Who do you **think** you are?

For parents to be, the to-do list never ends! There are books to read, nurseries to prepare, nappies, wipes, bottles and car seats to buy. But which job takes the most time? Which question consumes more mental energy than any other? *What name shall we give our child? What fits them? What sums up who they are and want to be?* No one gets to shirk this job. And everyone wants to get it right.

If a parent neglected to name their child we'd be surprised and concerned. After all, we don't number our children, we *name* them. 'What's your name?' is one of the first questions we'll ask in any social situation. In a new language we soon learn how to ask and answer the question. If someone said, 'I have no name', we'd ask if we'd wandered into a Marvel comic book. To have no name sounds completely unnatural. Why? Because our name speaks of who we are and of where we belong. Names make sense of people and of place. They're sometimes called handles, because they're something that we can grasp. Without a name, we can't be encountered or understood. Put simply, if you don't know what something is called, then you don't know what it is.

A name, then, is also a beginning. We see this in the book of Genesis. When God placed Adam in the Garden of Eden, his first job wasn't to start weeding or planting the crops. No, that came later. The first task Adam was given was to name what God had made. Humanity's 'dominion' over the world (Genesis 1) is demonstrated by Adam's naming of the world (Gen. 2). Once everything is named – and named correctly – the rest falls into place.

Genesis 2:19–20

'Whatever the man called each living creature, that was its name.' (v19)

For Prayer and reflection

Lord, thank You that You know us and have named us. Help us to see who we are in You and to live in the security and freedom that this brings. Amen.

The **power** of a name

Genesis 41:51–52

'Joseph named [him] Manasseh and said, "It is because God has made me forget all my trouble"' (v51)

I n Shakespeare's famous play, Juliet asks, 'what's in a name?' She's convinced that love will triumph over letters, but the play tells a different story. As comedy darkens into tragedy, the stage is littered with bodies. So what *is* in a name? Everything! Get it right and all is right with the world. Get it wrong and things fall apart. At school, we're taught about figures like Ivan 'the Terrible' and Alexander 'the Great'. Elvis was known as 'The King' and Diana as 'The People's Princess'. My daughter's favourite story is *Beauty and the Beast* where a girl called Belle redeems a man/beast called Adam. Their names say it all. In traditional cultures, names can describe the circumstances surrounding your birth. They take in the difficulties of your origins but they also cast a vision for how such pains might be redeemed.

In today's reading, Joseph names his sons to reflect his rise from the pit to the palace and from slavery to the highest office in the land. This redemption is expressed in the names of his sons. Manasseh means 'forget', Ephraim means 'fruitful'. For those who have endured deep suffering, we need both kinds of names: relief from the trauma; and assurance that the pain has been productive. As children of the great redeemer, we enjoy just this confidence. In Christ 'the old has gone, the new is here' (2 Cor. 5:17) and He makes us fruitful through our trials (John 15:1–2). I am Manasseh and Ephraim. You too. Whatever the world has called us, our identity given by Christ means redemption for yesterday and bright hope for tomorrow.

For Prayer and reflection

Lord, thank You that You redeem the old and turn the darkness and pain of the past into fruitfulness. Help me look beyond my present circumstances to these truths. Amen.

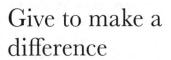

Give to make a difference

Our Bible reading notes are read by hundreds of thousands of people around the world. *Every Day with Jesus* and *Inspiring Women Every Day* are now free in the UK. We want everyone, whatever their financial means to have access to these resources that help them walk each day with our Saviour.

It makes all the difference. One reader in Malaysia said:

When I was first exposed to Every Day with Jesus about two years ago, I could sense something different, something refreshing, and I was energised. I used to struggle to translate knowledge into my daily life. EDWJ helped me to be more insightful, more positive, and to enjoy everyday life as a disciple. This helps me to be patient and positive at home, at work, and at church.

As we trust in God's provision, we know there are costs to providing this ministry. Can you give to make a difference in someone's life? Could supporting this vision be a way in which you serve?

A gift of just £2 a month from you will put daily Bible reading notes into the hands of at least one person who is hungry to know God and experience His presence every day.

Visit **wvly.org/donate** to give to make a difference, or use the form at the back of these notes.

The names we don't **choose**

Genesis 17:3–5

'No longer will you be called Abram' (v5)

Have you ever tried to give yourself a nickname? It almost never catches on. Names are something conferred by others – for better and for worse. Sometimes the names we are given are kind, and sometimes they hurt. Either way, they are hard to escape. In the words of Thomas C. Haliburton, 'Nicknames stick to people, and the most ridiculous are the most adhesive'. This has certainly been my experience! I was called 'Monkey Toes' as a child, and have been sensitive about my feet ever since. But of course it goes deeper than our looks. If we're called 'useless' or 'dull,' we'll feel – and act – useless or dull. If someone says we're precious and smart, we'll feel valued and act accordingly.

We all want to be named and seen; but it's also our greatest fear. What if we are called out? Will we be exposed and shamed? Or understood and accepted? How do you feel about the tags you've been given: the baby name you've outgrown; the nicknames that no longer fit? In the Bible, we see many examples of name changes. Abram became Abraham. It's a change from 'exalted father' to 'father of a multitude'. Given he was childless at the time, how must the name have felt? Absurd? A taunt? A rebuke? By faith, Abraham embraced the name *before* it described the reality. And this is our challenge too. God calls us 'righteous' in the midst of our sins. He calls us 'chosen' when we feel anything but choice. He calls us 'beloved' in the midst of our unloveliness and unlovingness. But God's name comes first, and our earthly reality catches up. Like Abraham, let's allow God's name to tell us who we really are.

For Prayer and reflection

Father God, thank You that You have a good purpose for me. Thank You that You know and love me personally. Help me to trust You today in every detail. Amen.

*wvly.org/iwed-mj22-3jun

Weekend

God's name for us fits

....

Genesis 17:5

'For I have made you a father of many nations.' (v5)

Names rub off on us. For instance, Scrivener means 'writer'. The 'royal scrivener' was the scribe at court. This is something my husband reminds me of, whether I'm publishing a blog or a book. 'Well done, love,' he'll say. 'Just remember: I made you a writer!' Technically he did. And, between us, maybe the name rubbed off on me!

When Abram became Abraham he was being called the 'father of a multitude'. From an earthly perspective this is a ridiculous name for a man who hadn't even fathered a child, let alone a clan, tribe or nation. But God's promises are always far in excess of mere human possibility. The Lord does not just promise the earth, He promises heaven – the prince of heaven Himself. In verse six, the 'kings' who are promised by God culminate in Christ. This is typical of God's grace: we have nothing; He promises everything – even His beloved Son. And after the name is given, it begins to rub off. Abraham acts like it. When you embrace it, a royal name begets royal behaviour.

....

Optional further reading

Genesis 17:1–27; 18:1–15; Psalm 72.

Names are a **gift**

Isaiah 42:1-4

'Here is my servant, whom I uphold, my chosen one in whom I delight' (v1)

Have you seen the TV shows where celebrities discover that they're related to kings and queens? Imagine that was you. You may be ashamed of who you are but suddenly you discover that you're royalty. You don't have to do anything to make this name yours. It's a *gift*, from someone who knows and cares for you deeply. This is the truth at the heart of the gospel. We're used to thinking that we make a name for ourselves through what we do. But the reverse is true. First we receive our identity and then we live out our calling.

This is the gospel and it's true for everyone, including God's own Son. Jesus submitted to the name given to Him by His Father; in fact, nothing could happen in His public ministry until He was named. The Gospels give us four eyewitness accounts of the life of Jesus, but each records the baptism of Jesus, though with different emphases. In Matthew's Gospel, we see how *public* was the naming of Jesus: the heavens are opened to all. In Luke it's more personal: *Jesus* sees into heaven and the Father says '*You* are my Son' (Luke 3:22, emphasis added). In Mark, we're shown how immediately Jesus goes from the baptism into the wilderness for His time of testing (Mark 1:9–12). In John, the spotlight is on the Spirit who comes down *to* Jesus as a dove so that *through* Him we all might be baptised (John 1:32–34). But in every account the identity of Jesus is central. The name of Jesus must be declared before the work of Jesus is performed. Maybe take some time to reflect on what this means for you?

For Prayer and reflection

Dear Lord, we thank You for Your Son, Jesus. May we know His identity and, before we do anything else, may we know it as *our* identity. Amen.

Belonging

In order to have a solid identity we need three things: to *belong*, to *be loved* and to *be liked*. We see this first at the baptism of Jesus, where there are three parts to the Father's words. First, the title: 'my Son'. Next, the security attached to this name: 'whom I love'. And finally, the sense of being personally known and valued: 'with you I am well pleased'.

We'll spend the next few days exploring this. Let's start with what it means to *belong*. Our culture tells us that if we can make ourselves acceptable, then we'll belong. This might sound appealing; especially if, like me, you're constantly seeking approval. But it's the wrong way round! Identity is found in community. I belong – and then I know acceptance and love. We don't find ourselves in isolation. Instead, we discover our identity in community, how we're known. Your legal name might be Jennifer Hannah Paterson. Yet, in practice, you're known as 'Jen' to your friends, 'Jenny' to acquaintances, 'Jennifer Hannah' to your mother, 'Honey' to your husband and 'Mrs Paterson' to your students. Names come out of relationship, and these relationships shine light on different facets of our character. However, the most important relationship we have is with our heavenly Father.

'Who am I?' is a good question. But far more important is 'whose am I?' I belong ultimately to my heavenly Father. And my home is with His Son. This is what it means to belong. Where do you feel you belong? How have you changed in order to 'fit in'? What was driving that? What difference does it make to know you belong with Jesus, no matter what?

Luke 3:21–22

'And a voice came from heaven: "You are my Son, whom I love; with you I am well pleased."' (v22)

For Prayer and reflection

Father, thank You that I will always have a place in Your kingdom and Your family. Help me to live as someone who belongs to You. Amen.

A name that's **beloved**

John 16:27

'The Father himself
loves you because
you have loved me
and have believed
that I came from
God.' (v27)

The comic, Dawn French, was once asked for the source of her confidence. She told this story about her dad. As a teenager, she was getting ready to go to her first disco but, unlike her friends, none of the boys had shown her any interest. Head down, she slunk towards the front door in make-up and tiny shorts. Her father stopped her and she steeled herself for a lecture about staying out late. But instead: He sat me down and told me that I was beautiful, that I was the most precious thing in his life, that he prized me above all else, and that he was proud to be my father. From that moment Dawn began to stop doubting herself. 'He succeeded in making my self-esteem so high', she said, 'that I wasn't going to let any boy kiss me at all that night. I was just too good!' Later she reflected, 'How wise of my father to say those words to me. It affected my whole life.' It's a powerful story and it illustrates a profound truth. Belonging, without love, brings slavery but belonging with love brings security. Ask yourself this question: What would it feel like to be 'sat down' by the ultimate Father and prized in this way? The Bible says this is the Christian's position. We hear the heavenly voice saying not only, 'You are my Son' but, 'You are my Son whom I love'. This is what makes us secure. Our earthly families may have hurt or disappointed us, but the Father of all loves us as He loves His Son. It's so incredible, I'll repeat it: *The Father loves us as He loves the Son.* Eternally, Jesus has been in the embrace of His Father (John 1:18, KJV). Now that's where we belong. It's where we're loved. It's home. What difference does it make to know that we not only belong, but are loved? How does unconditional love of a heavenly Father change how you see yourself?

**For Prayer
and reflection**

**Dear Father, thank
You for loving us as
You love Your own
Son. Please help
me to see others as
You do, and to love
them in the power
of Your Spirit.
Amen.**

A name that is **valued**

'Here is my servant,
   whom I uphold,
   my chosen one in
   whom I delight'
   (v1)

As we have seen over the last few days, our identity depends on being someone who belongs and someone who's beloved. Yet there's a piece of the puzzle that's still missing. It's not enough to be loved; we also want to be *liked*! Imagine if a father had seven sons and he called them all Matthew. They'd be confused and wounded. Why? Because we need to know that there's something special about us. We long to fit in; but we also want to stand out.

Our names are a mark of belonging and also of distinction. They remind us that we're personally known and personally *valued*. The Father tells his Son, 'With *you* I am well pleased' (Luke 3:22, emphasis added). Our key passage is the background to the Father's declaration at the baptism. Listen to how Jesus is described in verse one (ESV translation): 'Behold my servant, whom I uphold, my chosen, in whom my soul delights; I have put my Spirit upon him; he will bring forth justice to the nations'.

It's worth reading the whole of Isaiah 42 to see just how much the Father prizes his Son. The Father is not just pleased with Jesus in a general sense. He specifically lists the things that he *likes* about His Son. This reminds me of Ruby. She loves painting and will often bring me her creations. When I say, 'that's great', it's rarely enough. 'Why, Mummy?' she'll ask. '*Why* is it great?' That's the cry of my heart too. I want to be singled out, and I look to my Father for reassurance and approval. A good parent loves their children equally, but not interchangeably. Our *personal* name tells us that we are special; and that's why it sounds so sweet.

Father, I love Your Son for so many reasons [list them now]. Help me to know Your particular love for Jesus. And help me to know Your particular love for me. Amen.

A name that is **shared**

Hebrews 12:22

'But you have come to Mount Zion, to the city of the living God, the heavenly Jerusalem.' (v22a)

As natural children, we have no choice about what nation or family we belong to. Sometimes we're blessed with safety, love and security. Sometimes the reality is much darker. Through Jesus, however, there is hope. When we become Christians, we get a new birth certificate and become part of an eternal family – joined to Jesus and to other believers. As one body or Church, our head is the Lord Jesus Himself, and our names aren't just recorded on a paper register but in heaven! Church is where our knowledge of God gets explained, expanded and experienced. It's a family like no other and the only place where *everyone* belongs.

Of course, as with all families, this one isn't perfect. There will always be areas that can be improved and it's important to talk and pray these things through with each other. But just as Jesus committed Himself to an imperfect Church, so we are called to love and bear with one another. Even if you're completely unlike the others in your fellowship, you still belong. And the name we share is always greater than our differences.

Here are some of the reasons I go to church: because I can't love God till I know He loves me; to know who I am and where I belong; because the Bible tells me to (Heb. 10:24–25); to reflect on the week and see it through God's eyes; to gain hope and strength for what is ahead; to learn how to live and how to die; because the church is less when I'm not there; because we are one body; because everyone belongs; and because He is there. What reasons would you add as to why you go to church?

For Prayer and reflection

Bring to mind specific brothers and sisters from your church family in need of prayer. Bring their needs before God (and tell them you're doing it!).

Weekend

A new name from Jesus

....

Revelation 3:12

'I will write on them the name of my God… and I will also write on them my new name.' (v12)

You never forget your wedding day. The exchange of vows – and the joining together of two worlds; Emma Sloan to Emma Scrivener. When I married Glen, his name covered over mine. But something much better happened when I trusted Jesus. His glorious name covered my sinful one. Now, instead of being ashamed, I stand before heaven as righteous and spotless as Jesus Himself.

Jesus tells me this in the very last book of the Bible. He makes an incredible promise to those who trust in Him when He says, 'I will write on them my new name'. The name Jesus gives us is not like the new family name that I received when I got married. It's intimate, like a pet name, that's between you and your closest friend. It shows that God knows us completely – and it reminds us of our identity in Him. Best of all, it's a gift! We can't earn it. We can only receive it.

We don't find our true selves by becoming self-made men and women. And we're not at the mercy of other people's opinions. We receive our true identity from Jesus.

....

Optional further reading

Revelation 1–3.

A **(very) good** name

Genesis 1:26–31; 2:19–20

'Whatever the man called each living creature, that was its name.' (2:19)

W e're told in the very first chapter of the Bible that God is a naming God. He speaks creation into being. 'Light,' He says. And as He speaks it, the reality appears. As God makes His world He calls it 'day', 'night', 'sea', 'land' and eventually 'humankind'. But He employs adjectives as well as nouns. Each day He proclaims His world 'good'. On day six there's a difference: something is called 'very good'. It isn't the snow-capped mountains or the Andromeda galaxy. It's us: humans! God makes us in His image – and puts His name on us. This is an incredible act of protection and ownership. In contrast to what we might think or hear from others, it's God's name which tells us that we matter. He says we are 'very good'. In Genesis 1, God is the great namer. But in Genesis 2 God asks Adam to name the animals; a job He could easily have done for Himself. So why delegate? Because God is establishing a pattern.

As Adam names the creatures, he's demonstrating an understanding of their character and their place in the world – he's passing on God's blessing from on high. This is the flow: from heaven to humanity and from humanity to the ends of the earth, God's naming travels downhill. First, we take our identity from above and then in that security, we move out to understand our world.

If we don't understand our surroundings, if everything is bewildering and nothing seems to fit, if we know something's wrong but we can't put our finger on it, we have a naming problem. First, we need to call on the Lord and then seek His help in naming our world.

For Prayer and reflection

Father, we don't understand ourselves or our world. Show us the light and truth of Christ so that we may know ourselves and the world in which You've placed us. Amen.

Refusing the **gift**

Genesis 11:1–9

'Come, let us build
ourselves a city,
with a tower... so
that we may make
a name for
ourselves' (v4)

I f I asked you to complete the sentence, 'I am...' what would you say? If you answer 'clumsy', 'musical', ' a dog-lover' or 'vegan', you're probably a westerner. If you say, 'I am Rebekah's sister' or 'a Lopez' or 'Tony and Mary's daughter', then you might be from another culture.

In western cultures we often use personal names as a way of distinguishing ourselves from the 'herd'– but this is far from the norm. In Japan, for example, you put your family name first. It's a way of saying, I'm part of a larger unit – my family is who I am. In traditional cultures the temptation is to prize family and tribe so much that we depend on them for our sense of self. In individualistic cultures we're equally enslaved to an identity forged through ability and effort. But from a biblical perspective, they both involve 'trusting in the flesh.'

So what does this phrase mean, 'trusting in the flesh'? Our 'flesh' is our earthly and fallen nature; unleashed when Adam and Eve first disobeyed God. Put simply, we're looking for love (and identity) in all the wrong places. Some seek approval from family and community and others rely on their personal strengths. But as fallen humans we're trying to build a name from the bottom up, instead of accepting the name God gives us. It's an old, old temptation, pictured powerfully in this story in Genesis 11. There is a major problem with building a name from the bottom up. As the builders in Babel fired and pounded the clay to make bricks, so we pummel our flesh to forge an identity. And, as we'll see, all these efforts are starting in precisely the wrong place.

For Prayer and reflection

Father, forgive us for trying to make a name for ourselves, instead of receiving our identity from You. Remind us of who You are so we can see ourselves aright too. Amen.

'Otherwise we will be scattered over the face of the whole earth.' (v4)

Building my own name

O ur creator is a namer and He shares with us the privilege of naming His works. But whilst we call on His name, we don't name Him – and we don't name ourselves. That's the message of Genesis chapters 1–10. Sadly, in making an identity from below, the people of Babel do the exact opposite. The people of Babel refuse to receive from God or to reflect Him. Instead, they want to make names for themselves. This is living by the flesh. And we all do it.

Surrounded by images and names, we define ourselves by our achievements, our desires, our family, our jobs, our failures, our friends, our education – and the colour of our lipstick. These are as ephemeral as perfume ads; capturing our attention for a moment, then discarded and forgotten. So we move on to the next name, the next source of identity – anything that will tell us who we are and where we fit. Little wonder we're facing an identity crisis. The identities offered by our world seem glossy and out of reach. But here's a surprising truth: like reaching to the heavens and falling short, earthly names aren't *high* enough. They fall far short of the 'very good' identity that God has given us.

The builders of Babel wanted to have a tower with its head in the heavens. Members of the body of Christ have something even better. Our head, Jesus, really is in the clouds. As the head of the Church, He is at the right hand of the Father and in Him we have access to the throne room of the almighty (Eph. 2:6). It's not that Babel's builders were grasping at too much; they were grasping at too little. And it's our temptation too.

....

For Prayer and reflection

....

Dear Father, forgive us for trying to build our own names. Help us to know what we have in Jesus. Amen.

E-Learning Short Courses

Feed your mind in your own time and at a pace that suits you best. Ideal for individuals, small groups and congregations.

 **Insight Courses**

 **Paraclesis:**
A series on pastoral care

 **The Prayers of Jesus**

 **Eat, Pray, Share**

These and other courses are all available for you online at a price of £25 each.

To find out more and to buy a course, visit

wvly.org/online-courses

Giving yourself a **bad** name

Genesis 11:1–9

'Come, let us go down and confuse their language so they will not understand each other.' (v7)

There are many reasons why making a name for yourself is a bad idea. The prime reason is that it reverses the way God has intended things. He is the namer and we are the named. To try to establish our own identity under our own steam is to counter a divine flow from heaven to earth. But here is another reason why we should think twice before making a name for ourselves: in case it works!

The people of Babel want to build a tower to heaven and to make a name for themselves. They don't want to be dispersed across the earth but to stay in one place. But here's the irony: the people of Babel *do* make a name for themselves, but it's one of shame and mockery, as 'babblers'. They do indeed become people of renown, but what they are known for is rebellion and confusion.

In Genesis 1, God Himself walked with Adam, gave him a name and allowed him to name the animals. Genesis 11 is a complete reversal of Genesis 1. Instead of God walking with His people, they are separated from Him and try to build a tower to heaven. Instead of accepting and rejoicing in the name God has given them, they reject God and try to make a name for themselves. By naming the animals Adam reflected His Father and was able to give true names that expressed his understanding of himself, his Father and his world. But here, Babel's builders are separated from God, from creation and from one another. Instead of the words spoken in God's name with such power; their words have now become a babbling – a nonsense. When we want to gain an identity, sometimes the worst thing God can do is to let us have it!

For Prayer and reflection

Dear Father, we are sorry for trying to take Your place. We thank You that if we confess our sin, You will forgive us and make us clean again. Amen.

The **accuser**

Matthew 4:1–11

'The tempter came to him and said, "If you are the Son of God"' (v6)

A name can be a curse or a caress. It's the sweetest sound in the world, but it can also be the most terrifying. When used against us, names can hurt more than sticks and stones, and they leave unseen scars that may take a lifetime to heal. We've looked at the baptism of Jesus in Matthew 3, and why His public naming was so important. The Father uses it as a way of expressing His love for, approval of, and total confidence in, His Son. This is why the enemy attacks it, in the very next chapter, with that insinuation: 'f'.

Satan aims for the jugular – by attacking the *identity* of Jesus and casting doubt on the name *God* has for His Son. Even today, he uses the same tactics on God's people: by assailing us with false names and questioning our sonship. We see this in Revelation 12:10 where he is described as 'the accuser of our brothers and sisters, who accuses them before our God day and night'. In fact, the name Satan means 'accuser' and one of his favourite tactics is to condemn us by reminding us of our guilt and sin.

It's true that we are sinful and it's true that we are guilty, but in Jesus we have a new name and a new identity. In Him we can stand before the enemy and say, 'Jesus died and was raised to forgive my sins and to remove your accusations. In Him I stand and I am not condemned. His name is now my name and He intercedes for me.' When Satan tells us that we're not really believers or that we've done something that's too bad to be forgiven, we look from ourselves to Jesus. And the greater his accusations, the greater is Christ's grace.

For Prayer and reflection

Jesus, our sins are many and so are the enemy's accusations. But You died and were raised so that his names for us are no longer true. Help us to know this today. Amen.

Weekend

The defeat of shame

....

Revelation 12:10–12

'They triumphed over him by the blood of the Lamb and by the word of their testimony' (v11)

The Bible tells us that, as believers, our guilt and shame have been nailed to the cross. But as we saw yesterday, Satan, the father of lies, loves to call our new identity into question. Have you felt the whispers of his accusations? Call yourself a Christian? After what you did? How can you show your face after all you've done? How can you pray, after that?

How can we stand firm against Satan's accusations? Our key verse tells us: 'by the blood of the Lamb and by the word of their testimony'. 'The blood of the Lamb' means the sacrifice of Christ, our true Passover Lamb. Just as the lamb at Passover died in place of the firstborn son back in Exodus 12, so Jesus has died in our place, once and for all. When we bring to mind this sacrifice we gain victory over the accusations of the enemy.

The 'word of our testimony' also has power to oppose the accuser. We might not feel like we have a story or a gift for telling it. But every time we tell of the Jesus who saved us, we participate in His victory. There's power in the blood and power in the name, so let's speak it boldly.

....

Optional further reading

Revelation 12:1–17; 13:1–14:5; 19:1–21

The name of the **Father**

Exodus 33:18–20

'I will have compassion on whom I will have compassion.' (v19b)

How would you describe God? Powerful but aloof? Cuddly but ineffectual? Whatever you believe about Him, you can't escape God's name. But what *is* God's name, and how does *He* use it? This is the question that Moses asked in Exodus 33. So much depends on the answer. If God says His name is 'The Terminator', we're in big trouble. If He says, 'I am the Unknowable', we're orphans and the world is a frightening place. If He says, 'Call Me whatever you like,' He's either indifferent or ineffectual. So how does God respond to Moses? With goodness, mercy, and compassion (as our key verse highlights).

Moses was facing a lot and needed to know that God's presence would stay with them! Leading a grumbling multitude of Israelites through a wilderness for decades was not an enviable task. What did he need to know? He needed to know God. And who *is* God?

God is *good*: there is a radiant righteousness to the Lord who always does what is just. We never need to fear His 'dark side' – He doesn't have one.

God is *merciful*: He forgives our sins, removing them as far as the east is from the west. We never need to fear Him throwing our sins back at us. The wonderful truth is that he has forgotten them.

God is *compassionate*: He remembers that we are dust and comes to us always in stooping love: Psalm 18:35 tells us that God has 'stooped to make me great' (NCV). We never need to fear His condemnation. Christ has taken all our judgment and given us all God's grace. Here is a God to depend on, through any wilderness. As Psalm 9:10 puts it: 'Those who know your name trust in you'.

For Prayer and reflection

Thank You that You are a God who wants to know and be known by Your people. Amen.

No other name

Acts 4:8–13

'Salvation is found in no one else, for there is no other name… by which we must be saved.' (v12)

I n the old fairytale, Rumpelstiltskin, we learn the power of a name. If the heroine can guess what the imp is called, she will be spared from a terrible fate. The name unlocks great realities. The fairytale (as all fairytales do) reflects a deep truth. There is a name by which the heavens and the earth operate; a deep mystery. It is inscribed across the skies and the stars. To know it is to have the deepest realities of life and eternity unlocked. It is a mystery in that we must be told the name. But even the littlest child can know it. How? Must we spend hours scouring esoteric texts or climbing mountain peaks? No! There is just one essential requirement. We must come to Jesus as little children and simply receive it.

When the rulers of the Sanhedrin 'saw the courage of Peter and John and realized that they were unschooled, ordinary men, they were astonished and they took note that these men had been with Jesus' (v13). The mystery of mysteries is not plumbed by great scholarship or attained by high IQ. Being 'with Jesus' is the only prerequisite. And when we are with Jesus we realise the most profound truth: Jesus did not come to tell us *about* God – He *is* God, and He acts and speaks as the Lord Himself. To some, His name is 'honey in the mouth' (Bernard of Clairvaux). To others, it's the stench of death (2 Cor. 2:16). But to those who know *the* name, they have come to see the central truth of the cosmos: that all things make sense in *Jesus*. Without this name, everything is indistinct and we are lost in a fog. With this name, heaven, earth, life and eternity come into focus.

For Prayer and reflection

Father, focus our thoughts and affections on Your only Son, Jesus. May His precious name fill our mouths and lives. Amen.

His **beautiful** name

Isaiah 62:1–5

'You will be called
by a new name
that the mouth of
the LORD will
bestow.' (v2)

Weddings involve a joining of people, a joining of worlds, a joining of names. In Isaiah, we see the most beautiful wedding of all: the Lord Jesus to His bride. And as in so many earthly weddings, we see a new name bestowed. Hephzibah means 'my delight is in her'. Beulah means 'married'. So, just as a bridegroom rejoices over his bride, Jesus delights in us. But that's not all. Think of a royal wedding we might have seen – the marriage of Kate Middleton to Prince William. As the couple exchanged vows, Kate's life was transformed. She assumed not just William's name, but also all that belonged to him: his royal power, his royal status and his royal wealth. A nation watched transfixed as an ordinary girl became a princess.

The same thing happens when we are united to Jesus, but there's one crucial difference. At the cross, we don't just get what He has. For His part, Christ takes all that belongs to *us*: our mistakes and our weakness, our sin and our shame. Jesus gives us His riches and pays off our debts. He pledges Himself to us, 'for richer, for poorer, for better, for worse, in sickness and in health'. As we are joined to Him, we are given 'a new name that the mouth of the Lord will bestow' (v2). Those who were desolate and deserted (v4) find a home. Those who were shamed are publicly vindicated (v2). Our bridegroom rejoices in us!

In Jesus, whatever our history, it's as if we've never done anything wrong. In fact, it's as though we've always trusted and obeyed God perfectly. We might not feel like royalty, but we are. His name is ours.

For Prayer and reflection

Lord Jesus, we are united to You like a bride to a groom. You have our sins and we have Your righteousness. We are Yours and You are ours forever. We praise You!

Hallowing His name

Matthew 6:9–13

'This, then, is how you should pray: "Our Father in heaven, hallowed be your name"' (v9)

For many of us, this is a familiar prayer. We've taught our own children to say it every night. But because they know it so well, they race through it at a hundred miles an hour! As grown-ups we can do the same. So let's slow down for a moment and ask, what does it mean to hallow God's name? In Numbers 20:12, the Lord rebukes Moses and Aaron for not honouring Him as holy before the Israelites. Why? Because they 'did not trust in Him.' Hallowing God's name means actively trusting the Lord in daily life and acting on the basis of that trust.

A cricket fan might speak of the grass at Lord's Cricket Ground as 'hallowed turf'. What they mean is that it's special, different, set apart, unlike all other turf. In the same way, God's name can be set apart as special when His people act in line with His character. As believers, we are like letters written by God for others to read. When we behave badly or act as though we don't know Him, we are not simply disgracing our name, we are disgracing *His*.

This is a sobering truth. After all, as sinners, how can we ever show the holiness of God's name? Surely we're destined to fail! Yes. But we have a powerful Lord who works through broken people. He can show the beauty of His name even in our mess and our sin; because salvation is *His* work. God's holiness is displayed in His commitment to an imperfect Church, which still carries His name. We hallow Him, not by doing everything right, but by humbly accepting His word, admitting our mistakes and trusting in His Son Jesus as our Saviour. As we do this, His name is hallowed in our lives and in our hearts.

For Prayer and reflection

'Our Father in heaven, hallowed be your name' – in our lives, in our homes, in our churches and in our world. Amen.

The name we **carry**

Exodus 20:4–7

'You shall not misuse the name of the LORD your God' (v7)

Yesterday, we looked at the call to hallow God's name. It is described like this in the Ten Commandments: 'You shall not take the name of the LORD your God in vain' (ESV). We've talked about the name of the Lord, and what it entails to hold His name in disrespect or in vain. However, it's worth knowing that the Hebrew word for 'take' can also be translated 'bear'. So the command could read like this, 'do not bear the name of the Lord in vain'.

The implications of this are incredible. When we join God's family we not only take on His name, but carry it before the world. In this sense we are like God's ambassadors; not just in speech but in how we live and love. In ourselves, this is an impossible task! But as a community of redeemed sinners, we point away from ourselves and towards Jesus. He's a Saviour who comes to redeem all who turn to Him and we hold His Name out to a dying world. This is the role of the Church and it's been God's plan since the beginning.

In the Old Testament, the priests represent God to the people and the people to God. We see this in Exodus 28:29, when Aaron bears 'the names of the sons of Israel over his heart as a memorial before the Lord. But there's more. God not only puts His name on the people and blesses them Himself (Num. 6:22–27), He also calls His people to be His treasured possession and a kingdom of priests to the nations (Ex. 19:4–6)! This theme is repeated in John 17:11, as Jesus gives His name to the disciples and commissions them to carry it before the world. As God's people we take on His name and we bear it to the whole world.

For Prayer and reflection

Father, what an honour to bear Your name in this world! May we do so by pointing away from ourselves and to the beauty and love of Jesus, in whose name we pray. Amen.

Weekend

Suffering in His name

....

Matthew 10:22; Acts 5:41

'The apostles rejoic[ed] because they had been counted worthy of suffering disgrace for the Name.' (Acts 5:41)

How do we feel about bearing and wearing the name 'Christian?' It's one thing when we're with believing friends. But what about when the world treats Christ's name as a swear word? Or when the name of Jesus is precisely what brings difficulties into our lives? In Acts, the disciples have been lifting up the name of Jesus. They have healed in His name (3:6) and declared salvation in His name (4:10). But now they suffer in His name. It all goes together. But the apostles don't merely accept suffering, they rejoice in it. They were crucified, imprisoned, flogged and hounded. And the suffering is not a drawback, detracting from the joy they have in Jesus. It only increases their joy. How can this be? Because they know the 'fellowship of sharing in his sufferings' (Phil. 3:10). The name is sweeter in the midst of the pain. Perhaps take some time to listen to the song *Jesus, What a Beautiful Name*:*

Jesus, what a beautiful name

Son of God, Son of Man

Lamb that was slain

Joy and peace, strength and hope

Grace that blows all fear away,

Jesus, what a beautiful name.

....

Optional further reading

Acts 5:17–42; Philippians 3:1–10; Psalm 63

*Artist: Tanya Riches. Lyrics: Hillsong Music © 1995

Next Issue

JUL/AUG 2022

July

Trusting God in the Unexpected

······························

PAULA HALLIDAY

August

THE SWIFT AND THE BUTTERFLY

······························

SARAH GRACE

In **July**, Paula Halliday uncovers some beautiful truths and practical insights to help us see, seek and serve the Lord in the unexpected, often unwanted and uneasy, seasons of life.

In **August**, Sarah Grace helps us to reflect, consider and respond to how God may see us and how we consider ourselves and others. Gently challenging how we subconsciously perceive the world especially with regards to competition and comparison.

Available in a variety of formats

Get your copy from waverleyabbeyresources.org

His name is **becoming**

Revelation 3:12

'[Jesus said] I will write on them the name of my God… and I will also write on them my new name.' (v12)

I n all our studies we have been considering the 'new name' Christ gives us. This isn't a glossy promise or a grasping at what's out of reach. The new name is the real us. Saint Augustine writes of how, after becoming a believer, he ran into a former mistress on the street. Seeing her, he tried to flee. As she saw this she was shocked and cried, 'Augustine, it is I!' Augustine replied, 'Yes, but it is not I'. Meeting Jesus changed him; and it changes us forever too. Our new name reflects our new identity.

When you take on a new job or are given a new title, it can seem strange and overwhelming at first. Imagine you started at Tesco's unpacking boxes and now you're store manager! Often we suffer from imposter syndrome, doubting that we'll ever be able to match up. But gradually, these feelings change. We gain experience and grow into the role. Over time we're able to step up into something even bigger still.

Jesus calls us into a new name and title that's greater than we can imagine. It's a new name known only to you and it's the name of God Himself. No one could earn it or claim it in themselves, but it's a gift. And as we step into the identity He gives us, we can do so with confidence, knowing that we've been commissioned by the Father Himself. So, like the very best manager, Jesus knows us. He sees our potential and who we're capable of becoming. Left to ourselves, our capacity for selfishness and darkness is endless. But with Jesus as Lord, our capacity for glory is beyond our dreams. We are not our past or the judgments of others. We are who *He* declare us to be.

For Prayer and reflection

Lord Jesus, thank You for giving me Your name. Thank You that though I was once a beggar, now I reign with You. Amazing grace! Amen.

His name is a **process**

*T*he Repair Shop has been a surprise hit for BBC TV. But perhaps it's not so surprising. Restoration is a powerful idea. In the show, people bring old or broken items (usually with great sentimental value) to a skilled team of craftspeople. Incredibly, these experts are able to restore them, sometimes to a better condition than they were at the start. From music boxes to stopped clocks, a violin that survived a concentration camp to a treasured juke box, each object looks like junk, but to its owner it is priceless.

We carry stories, too – though some are too painful to recount. And like these heirlooms, we've seen better days. Some of us feel neglected or forgotten, battered by life and broken by our experiences. We can barely remember what we're here for or why we matter. And we've lost hope of any restoration. But restoration is what the Lord does. He doesn't just replace us with a new model. He redeems what is already there. Just as the broken body of Jesus was not discarded in the tomb but raised to resurrection glory, so God wants to work that very same miracle with all our lives.

We don't need to make ourselves a name, because we bear His. We don't need to prove ourselves because we are justified in the name of Jesus and by the Spirit of our God (1 Cor. 6:11). Yes, we are broken, but He is the master craftsman. He looks on us, the people He has made, and He writes His signature across us. He turns our brokenness into beauty and our stories into songs. For now, we're a work in progress! But one day He will restore us completely. And right now, He is at work in all of our mess.

Revelation 2:17

'I will give [them] a white stone, with a new name written on [it]' (v17b)

For Prayer and reflection

Father, thank You that, whatever our condition, we are not useless or cast off. You have written Your name across our scars and in Your eyes we are priceless. Amen.

His name is **better**

Isaiah 56:1–8

'I will give them an everlasting name that will endure for ever.' (v5)

So many of the names thrown at us are ugly – shameful names, self-hating names, humiliating names. We try to escape them by making new names for ourselves, but they are never enough. We can barely lift our eyes to one another, let alone to the heavens! Yet in our key verse we have an unbelievable promise: we're given 'an everlasting name that will not be cut off'. How is this possible? After all, the living God is perfect in glory, whilst we are clothed in dirt and shame.

This wonderful promise from Isaiah rests on that deep work of the suffering servant, prophesied in Isaiah 53. The promises of God are founded on the sacrifice of Christ. Are we ashamed of our nakedness? He was stripped naked for us. Are we feeling isolated or rejected? Even His friends scorned and betrayed Him. Are we tempted to give up? Jesus cries on the cross, 'Why have you abandoned me?' (Mark 15:34) Are we feeling bullied and persecuted? Jesus was hounded to the cross. Are we estranged from family and loved ones? Christ's own family and followers rejected Him. Are we desperate or overwhelmed? He asked of God in the Garden of Gethsemane, 'Is there any other way?' (Mark 14:36).

Whatever our uncleanness, His wounds and shame wash it away. We are changed: covered by His glory and His grace. Whatever we've done in the past, our shame is banished. Whatever we've been labelled, our disgrace is gone. Because of His suffering, we are healed. 'Instead of your shame you will receive a double portion, and instead of disgrace you will rejoice in your inheritance' (Is. 61:7). Thank You, Lord!

For Prayer and reflection

Dear God, thank You that You understand. Thank You for washing away my shame and healing what is broken. Amen.

Your new name

'I will proclaim the name of the LORD. Oh, praise the greatness of our God!' (v3)

Who am I? What makes me *me*? And how can I walk before heaven and earth with head held high? We all know that a good name is important. So, off we race, trying to make a name for ourselves. We define ourselves by our achievements, desires, ancestry, income, relationships, friends, education, wounds or worries. And yes, they can be significant, but they are not who we really are. Think back to Babel. We imagine that by making a name for ourselves we're aiming high, but in fact our ambitions are pathetically small. Sometimes it feels like we're on a never-ending cycle of self-improvement; building a name for ourselves that is never enough. But the one who made us offers us a cosmic name and a role that spans heavens and earth: to join in the divine nature; to marry the living God; to judge angels; to rule over all creation; to learn to live; and how to love.

No one in all creation has a name like the Lord. Here, Moses calls Him 'the Rock'. He is our Rock too. Reliable, trustworthy, solid, unmoving, strong and secure. Higher, greater and more beautiful than any other. Who knows what today and tomorrow may bring? Not us! Yet one thing is true. If we build upon His name we will stand firm, whatever we face. How sweet the Name of Jesus sounds - In a believer's ear! - It soothes his sorrow, heals his wounds, - And drives away his fear. - It makes the wounded spirit whole, - And calms the troubled breast; 'Tis manna to the hungry soul, - And to the weary rest. - Dear Name! the Rock on which we build; - Our shield and hiding-place; - Our never-failing treasury, filled - With boundless stores of grace.*

How Sweet the Name of Jesus Sounds: lyrics: John Newton; music: J.C. Lowry.
wvly.org/iwed-mj22-30jun

Lord Jesus, we praise You for Your beautiful and incomparable name. Thank You for sharing it with us. May we bear it rightly before a watching world. Amen.

Spiritual Formation

Spiritual Formation students at Waverley Abbey College grow in their understanding of who God made them to be and they become equipped to help others on their spiritual journeys.

Strengthen Your Core

In Search of Friendship

"Learning spiritual formation has broadened my concept of the heavenly Father and strengthened my faith by challenging what I believe God is doing in every part of life. God is good and this course helps us see our spiritual life more clearly."

Steve

For more information on our spiritual formation resources and courses please visit our websites

Resources – wvly.org/cl

Courses – wvly.org/sf-overview

Order form

Get Your **FREE** Daily Bible Reading Notes **TODAY! (UK ONLY)**

Your favourite Bible reading notes are now FREE. God has called us back to
the original vision of CWR to provide these notes to everyone who needs them,
regardless of their circumstance or ability to pay. It is our desire to see these daily
Bible reading notes used more widely, to see Christians grow in their relationship
with Jesus on a daily basis and to see Him reflected in their everyday living. Clearly
there are costs to provide this ministry and we are trusting in God's provision.

Could you be part of this vision? Do you have the desire to see lives transformed
through a relationship with Jesus? **A small donation from you of just £2 a month,
by direct debit, will make such a difference** Giving hope to someone in desperate
need whilst you too grow deeper in your own relationship with Jesus.

4 Easy Ways To Order

1. Visit our online store at **waverleyabbeyresources.org/store**
2. Send this form together with your payment to: **Waverley Abbey Trust, Waverley Abbey House, Waverley Lane, Farnham, Surrey GU9 8EP**
3. Phone in your credit card order: **01252 784700** (Mon–Fri, 9.30am – 4.30pm)
4. Visit a Christian bookshop

For a list of our National Distributors, who supply countries outside the UK, visit waverleyabbeyresources.org/distributors

Your Details (required for orders and donations)

Full Name: | ID No. (if known):

Home Address:

Postcode:

Telephone No. (for queries): | Email:

Publications

TITLE	QTY	PRICE	TOTAL
	TOTAL PUBLICATIONS		

UK P&P: up to £24.99 = **£2.99**; £25.00 and over = **FREE**

Elsewhere P&P: up to £10 = **£4.95**; £10.01 – £50 = **£6.95**; £50.01 – £99.99 = **£10**; £100 and over = **£30**

Total Publications and P&P (please allow 14 days for delivery) | **A** |

Payment Details

☐ I enclose a cheque made payable to CWR for the amount of: **£**

☐ Please charge my credit/debit card.

Cardholder's Name (in BLOCK CAPITALS)

Card No.

Expires End | Security Code

Continued overleaf >>

| **One off Special Gift to Waverley Abbey Trust** | ☐ Please send me an acknowledgement of my gift | **B** | |

GRAND TOTAL (Total of A & B)

Gift Aid (your home address required, see overleaf)

giftaid it I am a UK taxpayer and want CWR to reclaim the tax on all my donations for the four years prior to this yea **and on** all donations I make from the date of this Gift Aid declaration until further notice.*

Taxpayer's Full Name (in BLOCK CAPITALS) _____

Signature _____ **Date** _____

*I am a UK taxpayer and understand that if I pay less Income Tax and/or Capital Gains Tax than the amount of Gift Aid claimed on all my donations in that tax year it is my responsibility to pay any difference.

Your FREE Daily Bible Reading Notes Order

	Please Tick FREE	£2 pcm	£5 pcm	£10 pcm	Other
Every Day with Jesus	☐	☐	☐	☐	☐ £ ___
Large Print *Every Day with Jesus*	☐	☐	☐	☐	☐ £ ___
Inspiring Women Every Day	☐	☐	☐	☐	☐ £ ___

All CWR Bible reading notes are also available in single issue **ebook** and **email subscription** format. Visit **waverleyabbeyresources.org** for further info

CWR Instruction to your Bank or Building Society to pay by Direct Debit

DIREC Debi

Please fill in the form and send to: CWR, Waverley Abbey House, Waverley Lane, Farnham, Surrey GU9 8EP

Name and full postal address of your Bank or Building Society

To: The Manager _____ Bank/Building Society

Address _____

_____ Postcode _____

Name(s) of Account Holder(s)

_____

Branch Sort Code

| | | | | | |

Bank/Building Society Account Number

| | | | | | | | |

Originator's Identification Number

| 4 | 2 | 0 | 4 | 8 | 7 |

Reference

| | | | | | | | | | |

Instruction to your Bank or Building Society

Please pay CWR Direct Debits from the account detailed in this Instruc subject to the safeguards assured by the Direct Debit Guarantee. I understand that this Instruction may remain with CWR and, if so, deta will be passed electronically to my Bank/Building Society.

Signature(s)

_____

Date

_____

Banks and Building Societies may not accept Direct Debit Instructions for some types of account

For a subscription outside of the UK please visit www.waverleyabbeyresources.or where you will find a list of our national distributors.

How would you like to hear from us? We would love to keep you up to date on all aspects of the CWR ministry, including; new publications, events & courses as well as how you can support us.

If you **DO** want to hear from us on email, please tick here [ ] If you **DO NOT** want us to contact you by post, please tick her
You can update your preferences at any time by contacting our customer services team on 01252 784 700. You can view our privacy policy online at waverleyabbeyresources.org